CONTENTS

FREED-HARDEMAN
U N I V E R S I T Y

Our Identity

Freed-Hardeman University is an academic Community, associated with Churches of Christ, which is dedicated to providing excellent undergraduate, graduate, and professional programs.

Our Mission

The mission of Freed Hardeman University is to help students develop their God-given talents, for His glory by empowering them with an education that integrates Christian faith, scholarship, and service.

Our Values

Building on our heritage, Freed-Hardeman University will be the preferred academic community for students who seek to grow in faith, knowledge, and service in a changing world.

www.fhu.edu

INTRODUCTION

In 1975, my law partner and I were driving down River Road in Tuscaloosa, Alabama. Positioned there between River Road and the Black Warrior River is a lovely little lake.

As we passed by, I said to my partner, "I wonder who owns that beautiful little lake?" He replied, "The Lord does, He always has and always will."

I said, "Yes, I know the Lord owns the little lake, but do you know who holds title to the little lake?" He said, "The Lord originally held the title to the little lake when He made it and He will ultimately hold title to the little lake when it reverts back to Him at the second coming, so I would argue that the Lord holds title to the beautiful little lake."

By then we were both enjoying this little question and answer game. It is important for a lawyer to ask the right question in order to elicit the answer that he is seeking. So, I asked my partner one more question, "Do you know who is *presently* and *temporarily* exercising stewardship over the little lake?" To which he replied, "I have no idea."

The point of the story, "the parable," is this, while in this world we own absolutely nothing. We are temporary residents of this world, we are foreigners passing through. While we are on this earth, God entrusts to us a portion of His assets and charges us with the responsibility of being a good manager of His assets and to be ready at any time to give an accounting of our stewardship.

In a nutshell, that is the fundamental truth presented in this booklet. It is commonly known as the "Principle of Stewardship."

Amplifying the principle, we understand that a steward is simply a person who manages property that belongs to someone else. Good stewards always act in the owner's best interest, consulting and listening carefully to instructions from the owner in order to understand and implement his priorities. Our civil law requires that a steward must take extra special care of the property that he is managing for someone else, greater care than he would if the property were his own. A Christian must take extra special care of that which God entrusts to him.

An accurate understanding of stewardship and accountability will have massive, practical ramifications on a disciple's attitude and lifestyle regarding current income, accumulated assets, use of time, and use of unique talents. The concept of the godly steward lies at the very heart of the life of a Christian. Faithful stewardship is a foundational principle of the Christian life.

Stewardship cannot be relegated to a subcategory in the life of a Christian. It is comprehensive and involves every aspect of our being. It permeates every facet of the Christian's life. This includes our families, homes, businesses, time, abilities, relationships, jobs, and life opportunities.

> "Stewardship is nothing less than a complete lifestyle, a total accountability and responsibility before God. Stewardship is what we do after we say we believe, that is, after we give our love, loyalty, and trust to God, from whom each and every aspect of our lives comes as a gift." Ronald Vallet, author

> "The concept of the godly steward is not an add-on to the "proper" teaching on the life of the Christian, but instead it lies at its very heart. To be a Christian is to be a steward in the kingdom of the triune God of Grace." R. Scott Rodin, author

Becoming a faithful steward is essential to maturity in Christ. It demonstrates our respect for the Father's reign over every aspect of our lives. Stewardship is an act of obedience and submission. It is an act of worship.

It is a reflection of the Christian's whole spiritual condition. How we use His possessions for His glory is an accurate reflection of the condition of our soul. The goal of a steward is to "be found faithful" by his master. (1 Corinthians 4:2)

Over the years I have observed men and women who are earnest about their love and devotion to the Lord reach a "sticking" point or plateau in their relationship with God. They have experienced growth in faith, growth in the ability to verbalize their relationship with God, growth in knowledge of the scripture, growth in wisdom and discernment that come from living for Christ, growth in service, growth in sincerity and growth in love as Christ loved, but they are still stymied in the quest for a fuller relationship with God because they haven't grown in the grace of giving.

These Christians are out of round, like a tire with a flat spot. As they roll through life, they repeatedly hit that flat spot – k-thunk, k-thunk, k-thunk. When we release our grip on the assets entrusted to us by our Father, we experience release from the tenacious hold that greed and fear have on our hearts. Praise God for freedom to give and to be used by God - free "to grow in this grace also" (2 Corinthians 8:7). A selfish, tight fisted, possessive heart will hinder your whole Christian life.

Perhaps the problem is one of partial conversion, as Martin Luther states, "There are three conversions necessary [for the Christian life]: the conversion of the heart, the mind, and the purse."

It is the same problem experienced by the Rich Young Ruler (Matthew 19:16-26) who came to Jesus yearning to know what he must do to inherit eternal life. Jesus replied, "Keep the commandments." The young man exclaimed, "I have done all of these things, but I'm still empty and hollow. What's wrong? What lack I yet?"

Jesus answered, "If you wish to have perfection, spiritual maturity, and godly character, go and sell what you have and give the money to the poor, and you will have treasure in heaven." But when the young man heard this, he went away grieving and distressed, for he was very wealthy and he treasured his possessions more than his relationship with God.

Jesus said, "You haven't learned to give from your heart and to trust God to provide your needs. Why? Because of the grip that your wealth has on you." Sadly, men often refuse to come to grips with the truth that their trust, their source of security, is in their wealth and not in God. Often the inhibiting factor in our ability to develop trusting faith in God rests in this matter of stewardship.

Our proclivity is to trust in and lean on our own understanding and to rely on ourselves for security, to rely on our money. Our Lord wants us to rely on him, to permit him to direct our paths, to seek first His

Kingdom, His rule and reign over our lives and trust him to provide our needs. (Proverbs 3:5-6, Matthew 6:33, Philippians 4:19)

In the third chapter of Colossians, Paul describes a disciple of Jesus as one who has died to the things of the earth, one who has been raised to a new life in Christ with eyes fixed on things of heaven. Paul says Christians are to put to death sinful desires that lurk within the human heart such as sexual immorality, impurity, and lust. And then right after denouncing those abhorrent, earthy sins, he tightly links and condemns greed. "Do not be greedy, for a greedy person is an idolater, worshiping the things of this world." A greedy person is one who puts money above God, and that is idolatry. (Colossians 3:1-14)

Jehovah is not a killjoy. Far from it. He wants all of his children to live an abundant life, a life filled with happiness and unspeakable joy – joy that produces peace and contentment within the core of our being (John 10:10). Real joy comes from doing good, being rich in good deeds, being generous and willing to share, by laying up treasures in heaven, by taking hold of the life that is truly life (1 Timothy 6:17-19). It means doing nothing out of selfish ambition, considering others better than ourselves, and seeking the best interest of others (Philippians 2:1-4).

God set the supreme example of radical, sacrificial giving for his followers (John 3:16) by giving us his son. Our Lord Jesus was rich, yet for our sakes, he became poor, so that through his poverty we might become rich (2 Corinthians 8:8-9). Generous giving is God's method of leading us into a progressively deeper relationship with him, deeper dependence on him, and trust in his promises.

The remainder of the presentation is primarily an amplification of the principle of stewardship as applied to our accumulated assets, our estates. It begins with three Biblical truths:

1. Gods Owns Everything
2. We are God's Stewards
3. God Blesses Us So That We Can Bless Others

1 THREE FOUNDATIONAL PRINCIPLES AT THE HEART OF STEWARDSHIP

1. God Owns Everything

> "The earth is the Lord's, and everything in it.
> The world and all its people belong to him."
> Psalms 24:1

God created the rocks and the rills, the valleys and the hills, the sun and stars that shine, and the wealth in every mine. He owns the cattle on a thousand hills, all the animals in the forest, and every bird that flies. From everlasting to everlasting, the greatness and power and glory and majesty and splendor belong to the Lord of heaven and earth. (Leviticus 25:23; Deuteronomy 10:14; Job 41:11; Psalms 50:10; Haggai 2:8; Psalms 24:1; 1 Samuel 2:8; 1 Chronicles 29:10-11 & 14)

The Lord Jesus said that "all that belongs to the father is mine." The word "all" includes you and me. Not only do we belong to the Father and the Son because together they created all things (John 1:1-3), but Christians have been purchased from sin with the blood of Jesus and we are not our own (1 Corinthians 6:19-20), we belong to God (1 Peter 2:9-10). All other allegiances submit to God's new ownership. All that we are and have belong totally and completely to the Lord.

We sing, "This world is not my home, I'm just a passing thro. My treasures are laid up somewhere beyond the blue." Yes, Christians are pilgrims (one who journeys in a foreign land) (Hebrews 11:9-10 & 13-14), sojourners (a temporary resident) in an alien country. And, someday we will stand before the Creator and owner of all things and give an accounting of the resources entrusted to us by our Father (Matthew 25:14-30).

2. We Are God's Stewards

In the 25th chapter of Matthew, Jesus relates a parable about a Master who entrusted each of his servants with five talents, three talents, and one talent, respectively. Then, the Master left on a long journey and when he returned he required each servant to give an accounting of the talents that the Master had entrusted to each one. It is interesting to note that the servants considered that the original talents entrusted to them and the growth produced by wise investment belonged to the Master. (More on the Parable of the Talents in Chapter Four.)

That is the way it is with Christians. Christians belong to the Father. All that the Father has entrusted to us and all that we earn from the entrustment belong to our Father. All that we possess has been entrusted to us as his stewards. If we are faithful stewards, he will give us more to manage on his behalf. If we fail to be good stewards, he will remove his talents from our management.

3. God Blesses Us So That We Can Bless Others

Two parables told by Jesus, The Rich Man and Lazarus (Luke 16:19-31) and the Parable of the Rich Fool (Luke 12:13-21) contain strong warnings against greed and covetousness because a man's life does not consist of the things he possesses. Behind greed lies the four-letter word "self," and the absence of the seven letter word, "servant." No man enjoys rest for his soul, or peace, nor finds true life in possessions or even the abundance of earthly possessions. True life, true joy is derived from experiencing what Jesus intended when he said, "It is more blessed to give than to receive." (Acts 20:35)

This materialistic world in which we live is appealing and winsome. We are all so susceptible and vulnerable to the sins of greed and covetousness. That is why Jesus and his disciples frequently warned us against the folly of laying up treasures on earth. (Matthew 6:19-21; 1 Timothy 6:17-19) They knew that with clever worldly persuasion his disciples could be lured from their higher calling. The sights we see dazzle our eyes and the sounds we hear cause us to invest his entrustment in things that will not last. (2 Corinthians 4:18) The warnings were for them and for us.

In the process of living in this world we get confused and lose sight of stewardship. We emphasize accumulation. God emphasizes distribution. We emphasize ownership. God emphasizes stewardship. We talk about our possessions and assets. God talks about entrustment and stewardship of his assets.

With the assets that the Lord entrusts to us, he expects us to care for our families. "If anyone does not provide for his relatives, and especially for his immediate family, he has denied the faith and is worse than an unbeliever." (1 Timothy 5:8) He also expects us to pay our debts and instructs us to "Owe no man anything." (Romans 13:8) But he does not want us to strive for the things of this earth that non-Christians pursue. He wants us to seek first his kingdom and his righteousness and he will provide the food, clothing, and shelter that we need. (Matthew 6:25-34) The money God entrusts to us here on earth is eternal investment capital. Every day is an opportunity to buy up more shares in his kingdom.

Christ wants his disciples to tell the whole world the good news that Jesus came to seek and save men (Mark 16:15-16). He wants us to support the teaching of the gospel (Philippians 4:15-17; Romans 10:14-16) and give to those in need. (2 Corinthians 9:1-15; Ephesians 4:28; 2 Corinthians 8:7-9; James 1:27) God does not say that we cannot have money as a Christian but we cannot serve money as a god. He sternly warns us that loving money will lead us into all kinds of evil and many sorrows. (1 Timothy 6:10) The antidote that counteracts the love of money is to be rich in good deeds, to be generous, and willing to share.

> "In all of my years of service to my Lord, I have discovered a truth that has never failed and has never been compromised. That truth is that it is beyond the realm of possibilities that one has the ability to out give God. Even if I give the whole of my worth to Him, He will find a way to give back to me much more than I gave." — Charles Haddon Spurgeon (1834-92), English Baptist preacher

> "As base a thing as money often is, yet it can be transmuted into everlasting treasure. It can be converted into food for the hungry and clothing for the poor. It can keep a missionary actively winning lost men by the light of the gospel and thus transmute itself into heavenly values. Any temporal possession can be turned into everlasting wealth. Whatever is given to Christ is immediately touched with immortality." — A.W. Tozer (1897-1963), American pastor and writer

> "The best investment with the least risk and the greatest dividend is giving." — Sir John Templeton (1912-2008), investor and philanthropist

Giving is not man's plan for raising money, but God's plan for raising men and women. God does not need our gifts, but we need to give. We need to grow in the image of the Christ who gave His all for us and left us an example that we should walk in His steps.

We acknowledge God's ownership and our stewardship when we sing:

We give thee but thine own,
What ere that gift may be.
All that we have is thine alone,
A trust O Lord from thee.

2 WHAT ARE THE IMPLICATIONS OF GOD OWNING IT ALL?

In his fine book entitled, *Splitting Heirs*, Ron Blue lists three implications of God owning it all.

1. God can take back whatever He wants whenever He wants. We must hold all resources entrusted to us with an open hand. They don't belong to us. The question that we must continually ask ourselves is: How does God want me to use his resources?

2. Every spending decision is a spiritual decision. God has a plan for our lives (Ephesians 2:10) and he will provide the resources for us to accomplish his plan. He has not left us alone to make spending decisions. God has given us his Holy Spirit to guide us in wisdom, his Word as a source of truth, prayer as a constant source of communication with him, and a sound mind to help us spend his resources properly.

3. Stewardship cannot be faked. A person may be able to pray impressively, teach the Word persuasively, and sprinkle Christian jargon throughout his

conversation, but not be sincere. However, a person cannot fake stewardship. Your checkbook reveals the priorities in your life. It reveals how you use your time, where you live, how much debt you have, how much you save, how much you invest, how you dress, what you do for recreation, etc. Your checkbook reveals how you choose to use the resources entrusted to you by God.

In addition to Blue's thoughts, consider three lessons to be learned from a brief story in which Jesus observes offerings being made into the temple treasury by numerous rich people and by a poor widow. The contributions of the rich were obviously much greater than the contribution of the poor widow. From the human perspective, contributions made by the rich were impressive and deserved attention while the widow's contribution was insignificant and inconsequential. And yet, Jesus said the widow put more into the treasury than all the others. How could that be? It all depends on perspective – human perspective or God's perspective.

> [41]Jesus sat down opposite the place where the offerings were put and watched the crowd putting their money into the temple treasury. Many rich people threw in large amounts. [42]But a poor widow came and put in two very small copper coins, worth only a few cents.
>
> [43]Calling his disciples to him, Jesus said, "Truly I tell you, this poor widow has put more into the

treasury than all the others. [44]They all gave out of their wealth; but she, out of her poverty, put in everything—all she had to live on." Mark 12:41-44

From God's perspective:

1. Our giving is measured by proportion. He knows our portfolio. He knows our bank balance. He knows what we have and what we owe. We may impress other people by the extent of whatever it is we choose to do, but there is no way we could really impress God. "Each of you should give what you have decided in your heart to give, not reluctantly or under compulsion, for God loves a cheerful giver." (2 Corinthians 9:7)

2. Our giving is measured not by amount but by sacrifice. The rich gave what they would never miss, while this poor widow gave what she could not afford. From the human point of view, the widow's gift was irrelevant, but from God's point of view it was highly relevant and precious. The poor widow sacrificed and gave it all. And, that is what our Lord Jesus did for us. By implication, her gift reflects her dependence on her heavenly Father to supply her needs and to replenish her coffers so that she could give again. "And God will generously provide all you need. Then you will always have everything you need and plenty left over to share with others." (2 Corinthians 9:8, NLT)

3. Our giving is always in the sight of the Lord. "Jesus sat down…and watched." God sees into and searches our hearts. He knows our thoughts, intents, purposes, and motivations behind every action we take. Let us not look over our shoulder or around us to monitor what others may be giving. Instead, knowing that God knows everything about us, let us ask ourselves, "Have I ever really sacrificed in order to give to God?"

> "How I give is a measure of my faith in God. It is part of maturing in Christ. It is a form of worship that is part of my spiritual life. It is a reflection of my whole spiritual condition. God will judge us by the fruits of our lives, and how we use our possessions is a more accurate reflection of the maturity and condition of our soul than the underlining in our Bible." Paul Hubble, Industrial Engineer for Boeing Company

Lord, give us the ability at all times to see all things from your perspective. And then, give us the courage and conviction to trust and to obey.

3 THE "SELF-MADE" MAN SIN

In the 8th Chapter of Deuteronomy, God is preparing to lead the Children of Israel into the Land of Promise to occupy cities that they did not build, to live in houses they did not construct, to drink from wells they did not dig, and to feast from vineyards and olive groves they did not plant. He had led them through the desert for 40 years. During that time, he fed them with manna from heaven and quenched their thirst with water from a rock. He comforted them with his continual presence and guided them with a pillar of fire by night and a pillar of cloud by day. Their clothes did not wear out and their feet did not swell. He did this to humble them, to test them, and to cause them to put their total trust in him.

God knew their haughty and prideful hearts, so as he was about to bring them into the land, he admonished them to revere the Lord, to keep his commands, and walk in his ways. He said, "I know you. I know your heart. When you have feasted on the wheat and barley, and figs, and pomegranates, and honey, and bread and are satisfied – do not forget the Lord! Give him praise and observe his commands and decrees." If you fail to remember God and praise him for these gifts then, this is what will happen:

> [12]...when you eat and are satisfied, when you build fine houses and settle down, [13]and when your herds and flocks grow large and your silver and gold increase and all you have is multiplied, [14]then your heart will become proud and you will forget the LORD your God, who brought you out of Egypt, out of the land of slavery. [15]He led you through the vast and dreadful wilderness, that thirsty and waterless land, with its venomous snakes and scorpions. He brought you water out of hard rock. [16]He gave you manna to eat in the wilderness, something your ancestors had never known, to humble and test you so that in the end it might go well with you. (Deuteronomy 8:12-16)

This chapter in Deuteronomy is one of the most contemporary passages in the Old Testament. Why? Because, the nature of man has not changed. These words describe the nature of man in past generations, in the present generation, and in all future generations. They were and we are so vulnerable to pride.

In ancient Babylon, there lived a King named Nebuchadnezzar. He ruled a vast kingdom, lived an opulent lifestyle, and was exceedingly proud. He believed that this extraordinary prosperity was due entirely to his great leadership. One night, he had a deeply disturbing dream that only Daniel, through the power of Jehovah, could interpret. (Daniel 4) The dream was about an enormous, magnificent tree that provided food and shelter for all inhabitants of the kingdom. Then a holy messenger came down from heaven and commanded that the tree be cut down leaving only a stump. As he watched, the stump transmuted into a wild beast of a man driven from mankind and compelled to dwell with animals in the fields.

With great trepidation, Daniel warned Nebuchadnezzar that this stump was his future unless he humbled himself and recognized that "the Most High is ruler over the entire realm of mankind, and He bestows kingdoms and authority on whomever He wishes." Nebuchadnezzar failed to heed the warning. One year later in the midst of a display of arrogance, the prophesy was fulfilled. His royal authority was taken from him and he was driven away to eat grass and live with the wild animals. His hair grew like the feathers of an eagle and his nails like the claws of a bird.

After a period of time, Nebuchadnezzar lifted his eyes to heaven and his sanity was restored. He praised, honored and glorified God and acknowledged Jehovah's eternal, sovereign dominion over all kingdoms of the earth. And he learned his lesson, "those who walk in pride he is able to humble." (Daniel 4:37)

In spite of our knowledge and understanding that all we have is a gift from God, nevertheless, we, like Nebuchadnezzar, assume that our big houses, our fancy furniture, our expensive cars, our fine jobs, our IRA's, our stocks, our bonds, etc. are all due exclusively to our own ingenuity and resourcefulness. Some have said, "By the labor of my hands, by the sweat of my brow, and by my clever wit, I have produced and acquired these things, and they are mine." God speaks directly and specifically to that self-sufficient attitude of the self-made man in Deuteronomy 8:17.

> "You may say to yourself, 'my power, and the strength of my hands have produced this wealth for me!' But remember the Lord your God, for it is he who gives you the ability to produce wealth." (Ability - talent, time, and/or treasure entrusted to us by Jehovah that we are privileged to oversee for his glory.)

When gratitude, appreciation, thankfulness, and thoughtfulness are low, forgetfulness is high, selfishness abounds, and pride swells our heads and clouds our minds. When this happens, God is absent from our hearts and our plans. Far too often, abundant blessings produce complacency, arrogance, self-reliance, and selfishness.

The prophet Hosea reinforces the lessons from Deuteronomy, "When I fed them, they were satisfied;

when they were satisfied, they became proud; then they forgot me." (Hosea 13:6) That's always the danger— to look at all that God has given us and start to think, "This is about us." We begin to believe that somehow we deserve all that we have instead of acknowledging the sovereign grace of God that has put these good things into our hands. So, let's be conscious that our prosperity results from His abundant blessings. The only way to survive prosperity is to see it as a gift from God's hand, and to use it generously to help other people.

In his first letter to his brothers and sisters in Corinth, Paul asked them and us a rhetorical question. "What do you have that you did not receive? And if you did receive it, why do you boast as though you did not?" (1 Corinthians 4:7)

4 PARABLE OF THE TALENTS

Like the men in the parable of the talents, we have been entrusted with talents (units of money) in varying degrees and charged with the inescapable obligation to give an accounting to our Heavenly Father of all money with which we have been entrusted.

> [14]"For it will be as when a man going on a journey called his servants and entrusted to them his property; [15]to one he gave five talents (five units of money), to another two, to another one, to each according to his ability. Then he went away.
>
> [16]He who had received the five talents went at once and traded with them; and he made five talents more. [17]So also, he who had the two talents made two talents more. [18]But he who had received the one talent went and dug in the ground and hid his master's money.
>
> [19]Now after a long time the master of those servants came and settled accounts with

them. ²⁰And he who had received the five talents came forward, bringing five talents more, saying, 'Master, you delivered to me five talents; here I have made five talents more.'

²¹His master said to him, 'Well done, good and faithful servant; you have been faithful over a little, I will set you over much; enter into the joy of your master.'

²²And he also who had the two talents came forward, saying, 'Master, you delivered to me two talents; here I have made two talents more.'

²³His master said to him, 'Well done, good and faithful servant; you have been faithful over a little, I will set you over much; enter into the joy of your master.'

²⁴He also who had received the one talent came forward, saying, 'Master, I knew you to be a hard man, reaping where you did not sow, and gathering where you did not winnow; ²⁵so I was afraid, and I went and hid your talent in the ground. Here you have what is yours.'

²⁶But his master answered him, 'You wicked and slothful servant! You knew that I reap where I have not sowed, and gather where I have not winnowed? ²⁷Then you ought to have invested my money with the bankers, and at my coming

I should have received what was my own with interest.

²⁸So take the talent from him, and give it to him who has the ten talents. ²⁹For to everyone who has will more be given, and he will have abundance; but from him who has not, even what he has will be taken away. ³⁰And cast the worthless servant into the outer darkness; there men will weep and gnash their teeth.' Matthew 25:14-30

When studying this passage, some interpret "talent" as a natural ability or aptitude, and then emphasize that:

1. we must use our talents,
2. when we use them, we will be given more talents, and
3. if we fail to use them, we will lose them.

Those conclusions are correct with regard to a natural ability, but in this parable the meaning of "talent" is clearly money. So, let's focus on other equally valid truths from this passage.

The text teaches that we will all stand before God and give an accounting of:

1. the original assets with which we have been entrusted and
2. the earnings from the original assets.

Neither the original money given to us by the Father

nor the increase produced by using that money belongs to you or to me to do with it as we please. We are to invest the Master's money for the Master's benefit.

We have been instructed and admonished from the pulpit on our individual responsibility and privilege of giving liberally, cheerfully, sacrificially and purposefully of the first fruits of our current income and that is well and good. We need more teaching on this, not less. But we seldom hear teaching from God's word on stewardship of our estates. Somehow we have taken the scriptural teaching on giving of our current income and concluded that everything that is left over after we give our weekly contribution is ours. In addition, we arrogantly and erroneously conclude that everything that we save and accumulate is ours to do with as we please without responsibility or accountability to God.

Fellow pilgrims, that is not true. The one who owns the sheep owns the wool. The parable of the talents teaches that we will give an accounting to God of the original asset and the income it generates. The "Greatest Generation" and the "Baby Boomers" have accumulated assets through God's blessings. They have worked hard, been frugal, and their assets have appreciated. As a result, Christians now have estates. Regrettably, we have not had much training from our ancestors concerning our responsibility toward the Lord from our estates.

The stewardship of accumulated possessions has seldom been mentioned and very rarely emphasized from pulpits. In the past, with few exceptions, teaching on stewardship of our estates has not been needed. Sixty or seventy years ago, sermons on this topic were not preached because only a few of God's people had estates. When Uncle Jim died, the question was, "Who will help bury Uncle Jim and pay his debts." There was no question about the distribution of his assets because he had no assets. Today we have estates. Today we need to hear the Word of God on this question. Through frugality and appreciation of assets, our brethren have accumulated assets and now need to examine the scripture concerning God's reign over our assets, businesses, professions, and investments.

5 PARABLE OF THE RICH FOOL

At the time of our death, the things that we have stored up constitute our estate. The challenge for each of us is to introspectively ponder whether or not we have planned our estates in such a way that we can stand before the Lord with confidence that we have been good stewards of His assets. Christians must ask themselves, "Whose shall these things be after I'm gone? Will they be used for the glory and honor of our Lord, for the advancement of His kingdom or will they be used to strengthen the kingdom of Satan." We cannot have it both ways.

At the beginning of Luke, Chapter 12, Jesus is surrounded by thousands of people. Why had they come to see and to hear Jesus?

1. Curiosity, "Who is this man? Could he be the Messiah?"
2. Many came to be healed of diseases, and
3. Others came out of a holy hunger for peace, contentment and relief from the oppressive burdens

of life under Roman rule.

One man was there with his own private agenda. His own selfishness, greed and covetousness drove him to Jesus. He was seeking someone in authority to rule in his favor, to side with him against his brother. While Jesus was addressing the multitude on eternal principles, this man, who was obviously concerned with nothing but himself and his rights, rudely interrupted Jesus with this demand, "Teacher, tell my brother to divide the inheritance with me."

We know the dispute between the man and his brother concerned their father's estate. We do not know whether this man was right according to the law or whether his brother was right. The man believed that his brother was treating him unfairly in the distribution of his father's assets. He had come to Jesus seeking justice on an earthly issue.

Jesus seems to be a bit put out with this man's discourteous interruption but more disturbed with this man's attitude of selfishness, covetousness and greed. He could read the man's motives and the thoughts and intents of his heart. Jesus said to him, "Man, who appointed me a judge or arbiter between you?"

Now, let's examine the rest of this familiar story found in the 12th Chapter of Luke. It is entitled the Parable of the Rich Fool and is found in verses 13-21, just 9 verses.

As you read these few verses, notice the number of times that the rich man uses the pronoun "my" and "mine" and especially the perpendicular pronoun "I". This fool was wrapped tightly within himself. William Barkley writes, "It was said of a self-centered young lady, 'Edith lived in a little world, bounded on the north, south, east and west by Edith.'" That seems to be a good description of this man.

In these nine verses there are fifteen personal pronouns – references to self. This passage will take on greater meaning for you if you will personalize it by mentally substituting your name for the rich man.

> [13]Someone in the crowd said to him, "Teacher, tell my brother to divide the inheritance with me."
>
> [14]Jesus replied, "Man, who appointed me a judge or an arbiter between you?" [15]Then he said to them, "Watch out! Be on your guard against all kinds of greed; life does not consist in an abundance of possessions."
>
> [16]And he told them this parable: "The ground of a certain rich man yielded an abundant harvest. [17]He thought to himself, 'What shall I do? I have no place to store my crops.'
>
> [18]"Then he said, 'This is what I'll do. I will tear down my barns and build bigger ones, and there I will store my surplus grain. [19]And I'll say to

myself, "You have plenty of grain laid up for many years. Take life easy; eat, drink and be merry."'

[20]"But God said to him, 'You fool! This very night your life will be demanded from you. Then who will get what you have prepared for yourself?'

[21]"This is how it will be with whoever stores up things for themselves but is not rich toward God." (Luke 12:13-21)

In Verse 15, Jesus turned and addressed "them", "the rest," "the multitude" and used this event to teach another powerful spiritual lesson. "Take heed," "Beware," "Watch out," "Be on your guard" against greed and covetousness because a man's life does not consist of the things he possesses even if he has an abundance of possessions.

Greed is an inordinate, relentless desire for more...
_____ . (You fill in the blank. What is it for you? Is it money, stocks, land, power, cars, boats, houses, clothes, vacations,…?) Greed is forever craving, grasping, wishing, wanting, and striving for more. Greed is always seeking and searching for that elusive something that will bring satisfaction. Greed is forever discontent. Greed is raw, unchecked materialism. Accumulating the treasures of this world leaves us empty and unsatisfied. Why? Because, "You have made us for yourself, and our hearts are restless until they rest in thee." Augustine

The siren call of materialism constantly bombards us from every billboard, in every magazine, in every commercial on TV, on our laptops and phones. It is impossible to escape these alluring appeals. Advertisements are designed to make us discontent, restless, and unhappy with what we have, the way we look, and the way we feel. And suggest that if we purchase the product then serenity, tranquility, and joy will be ours. We (including me) are so vulnerable and gullible.

With these words, the English poet, William Wordsworth, warns against being absorbed by materialism and thereby distancing oneself from God's creation.

"The world is too much with us; late and soon,
Getting and spending, we lay waste our powers;"

John Stott, gave us good advice when he said, "We should travel light and live simply. Our enemy is not possessions but excess."

In this parable, Jesus labels this rich man a "fool." He told this parable for the benefit of the man, the multitude and for you and me. Why? Because we are all so susceptible and vulnerable to the sins of greed and covetousness.

There is nothing wrong with being rich. It is dangerous, but not wrong. The farmer is not being condemned for being successful. There is nothing wrong with reaping a rich harvest. Neither is there a hint that the farmer was dishonest, or that he had received his wealth in an unscrupulous manner. The man just wanted a little more, a little more for himself, a little more to sustain the lifestyle to which he had become accustomed.

Someone once asked John D. Rockefeller what it would take to satisfy a man and his answer was profound. "A little bit more than he has." That is how much it will take to satisfy you and me if we are trying to find satisfaction in things—money, fame or control. If that is your standard, you will never find peace.

Jesus said that it is harder for a camel to go through the eye of a needle than it is for a rich man to enter the Kingdom of God. (Matthew 19:16-30) From the viewpoint of man, it is impossible for a camel to pass through the eye of a needle, so it must be impossible for a rich man to enter the Kingdom of God. Jesus agreed with that conclusion, but he said, "With man this is impossible, but with God all things are possible."

Some of God's choicest servants were very rich: Job, a perfect and upright man who feared Jehovah and hated evil (Job 1:1), Abraham, father of the faithful and a friend of God (Romans 4, Galatians 3, James 2:23), David, a man after God's own heart. David is an example of one who planned to include God in his estate. He designed the Temple and worked diligently so that Solomon could build it. Although he was not permitted to build the Temple, he gave generously from his accumulated assets to be used after his death in the construction of the Temple (1 Chronicles 28 & 29). These men were blessed with enormous wealth and they used their wealth to bless others.

There is nothing wrong with tearing down old barns and building bigger barns if the goal is to protect and preserve blessings from God so that they can be used to advance the Kingdom, help the needy, and glorify the Lord. That is good stewardship.

Incidentally, why do we work? Among many, here are four reasons.

1. To care for our families. "If anyone does not provide for his relatives, and especially for his immediate family, he has denied the faith and is worse than an unbeliever." (1 Timothy 5:8)

2. To pay our debts. "Owe no man anything." (Romans 13:8)

3. To support the teaching of the gospel. (Galatians 6:6, 3 John 5-8, 1 Corinthians 9, Philippians 1:3-5, 4:10, 15-16; 2 Corinthians 11:8-9, Romans 10:13-15)

4. To have to give. "Let him that stole steal no more, but let him labor, working with his hands the thing which is good that he may have to give to him that has need." (Ephesians 4:28)

We know these principles and must not forget them lest we, like the Rich Fool, live our lives with little or no regard for God. The Rich Fool had no room in his life for God. He totally left God out of his life, out of his plans. When we leave God out of our plans, we will build bigger barns. We will store up treasures on this earth where moths and rust corrupt and where thieves break through and steal. (Matthew 6:19-21)

It is really a foolish way to live. Why? Because, it is a bad investment. It is a "short-term" investment. Virtually, every investment manager advises his or her clients to make long-term investments, but every investment in this world is a short-term investment. That's why Jesus commands us "lay-up treasures in heaven." That is truly a long-term investment, an investment that will last for eternity.

All of us have hopes and dreams for life. We long to play the game to win, but often the life we want seems to slip from our grasp. We lose sight of what is truly important and expend our energy on things that merely go back in the box when the game is over. That's why the message of Psalm 90 is so important for us to take to heart: "Teach us to number our days aright, that we may gain a heart of wisdom." (Psalm 90:12)

This world is going to pass away. Our purpose in this life is to prepare to live throughout eternity with our loving Father, our Savior, and the Holy Spirit. We were not made to last forever, and God wants us to be with Him in Heaven. Rick Warren once said, "One day my heart is going to stop, and that will be the end of my body - but not the end of me. I may live 60 to 100 years on earth, but I am going to spend trillions of years in eternity. This is the warm-up act - the dress rehearsal. God wants us to lay up treasures in heaven for our use throughout eternity."

The rich fool depended on himself and his riches. Sadly, he thought he was secure and self-sufficient; but there is no true security except in the Lord. He thought that he was in full control, that everything he had belonged exclusively to him, and he intended to consume it entirely upon himself in riotous living.

Looking back at verse 20, we see that the rich man speaks no more. God speaks last. God always speaks last.

Jesus tells us never to call a man a fool and yet he called this man a fool. With this story, Jesus demonstrated the folly of the rich man's life – the absolute folly, the stupidity of depending on earthly riches. After calling this man a fool, Jesus said, "and so is he." (KJV) So is he what? A fool who lays up treasures for himself and is not rich toward God. God told this rich man that he would die that very night, but said, first I want to ask you a question, "And then, whose shall these things be?"

Dietrich Bonhoeffer, wrote that the first call on a Christian's life is "the call to abandon the attachments to this world." The "rich fool" certainly had not abandoned his strong attachment to this world. Have I? Have you abandoned your attachments to this world?

"He is no fool who gives what he cannot keep to gain that which he cannot lose." Jim Elliott, missionary and martyr.

Only one life, yes only one,
Soon will its fleeting hours be done;
Then, in 'that day' my Lord to meet,
And stand before His Judgement seat;
Only one life, 'twill soon be past,
Only what's done for Christ will last.

Only one life, a few brief years,
Each with its burdens, hopes, and fears;
Each with its clays I must fulfill.
living for self or in His will;
Only one life, 'twill soon be past,
Only what's done for Christ will last.

C.T. Studd, missionary

6 APPLICATION

Have you made provisions for a portion of the assets entrusted to you to be used after your death for the advancement of Christ's Kingdom, for good works, and for the glory of the Lord? Statistics tell us that 50-70% of our population die without a valid Last Will and Testament. My experience tells me that the numbers are no better among disciples of Christ.

If you have not planned your estate and reduced your plan to valid and enforceable testamentary documents, then you are forfeiting your privilege of thoughtfully and prayerfully dedicating a portion of your estate to good works. You have abdicated your responsibility of being "rich toward God?" To what extent have you been seeking to live a life that is rich in God's eyes? How might you resolve to change this in the future?

If you do not have a valid estate plan, the state in which you live has made a will for you. Every state has its law of Descent and Distribution. None of those laws provide for a gift to advance the Lord's work. Again, studies tell us that the average person spends about 85,000 hours accumulating assets and about 2 hours preparing for the distribution of those assets. On its face, that is poor stewardship.

What about you and your estate? "Whose shall these things be" when you die?

A. Two Families – Most disciples of Christ have TWO FAMILIES, one temporary and one eternal:

1. Your PHYSICAL FAMILY – We are charged with the responsibility to provide for the earthly needs of our physical families, especially our spouse and our minor children. You need to provide for your physical family in your will—at least until they are able to take care of themselves.

> "But those who won't care for their own relatives, especially those living in the same household, have denied what we believe. Such people are worse than unbelievers." (1 Timothy 5:8)

2. Your SPIRITUAL FAMILY—the word of God teaches clearly that our relationship to our spiritual family takes precedence over and is more important than our relationship to our physical family.

Jesus said,

> "He who loves Father, Mother, son or daughter more than me is not worthy of me." (Matthew 10:37)

"[46]While Jesus was still talking to the crowd, his mother and brothers stood outside, wanting to speak to him. [47]Someone told him, "Your mother and brothers are standing outside, wanting to speak to you." [48]He replied to him, "Who is my mother, and who are my brothers?" [49]Pointing to his disciples, he said, "Here are my mother and my brothers. [50]For whoever does the will of my Father in heaven is my brother and sister and mother." (Matthew 12:46-50)

Christians should provide for the growth and nurture of their physical families and their spiritual families through their estate plan, but that general statement is subject to many variations depending on the facts and circumstances confronting each individual.

No one can tell you how to divide your estate between your physical family and your spiritual family. Each of us has a different, a unique situation. Those with young children have a different situation from those whose children are grown and are able to take care of themselves. This is a matter that must be considered carefully and prayerfully.

In my experience, I have found that people wrestle mightily with Two Very Difficult Problems:

1. Children Living in Rebellion to God – For a Christian this problem requires a grave and difficult decision. Bequests from your estate will be used to

advance the cause of Christ or used to oppose Christ. If you leave gifts to a child who is living in total disregard for God, how will your assets be used after you are gone?

Jesus said, "He that is not with me is against me; and he who does not gather with me scatters abroad." (Matthew 12:30)

If that is your situation, pray that God will give you wisdom, courage and strength to make the right decision.

Christians believe that the convicting power of the Gospel can produce genuine change in the hearts, minds, and conduct of men and women. For those that we love, we constantly live with the hope and prayer that they will yield their hearts and submit their wills to the sovereign God, that they will put their faith in Him and be immersed in His cleansing blood. If you have unbelieving children who are living in rebellion to God, perhaps a well-crafted trust with appropriate conditions to the receipt of benefits would be useful in implementing your desires for your child and your estate.

2. Great Wealth – If you have been blessed with great wealth and possessions, then you must decide how wealthy you want to make your children. Will it be in the best interest of the souls of your children to make them wealthy? You have worked long and struggled

hard to build your estate, and in the process you have developed character, integrity, honesty, and learned the value of hard work. If you give your children too much, you may deprive them of the opportunity to build character, integrity, honesty, and to learn the value of hard work.

It is not wise to leave your children with great wealth if they have not been thoroughly schooled in the biblical perspective on money and how to properly manage it. Very few people can live in the lap of luxury and maintain the values, priorities, and the inner spiritual dynamics of true Christianity. It is wise to inculcate within your children Biblical wisdom concerning God's teaching on stewardship before transferring wealth to them.

Men of wisdom and wealth have this advice:

Warren Buffet, "Parents should leave children enough money so that they would feel they could do anything, but not so much that they could do nothing."

Bernard Marcus, "An inheritance can be a terrible burden for some. If my kids want to get rich, they'll have to work for it."

Michael Bloomberg, "I have no intention of cutting them out; the question is how much to give them so as not to hurt them."

Andrew Carnegie, "The almighty dollar bequeathed to a child is an almighty curse. No man has the right to handicap his son with such a burden as great wealth. He must face this question squarely: Will my fortune be safe with my boy, and will my boy be safe with my fortune?"

Thomas Carlyle, "Adversity is sometimes hard upon a man; but for one man who can stand prosperity, there are a hundred that will stand adversity."

Commodore Vanderbilt, "Inherited wealth is as certain death to ambition as cocaine is to morality."

Henry Ford, "Fortunes tend to self-destruction by destroying those who inherit them."

John Ortberg, "The only real thing we can count on to measure eternal worth is the relationship we have with Jesus Christ. Life, no matter how we play it, will not go on forever. When the game is over it's all going to end up in the same place. As an ancient Italian proverb put it: "Pawn and king alike, they all go back in the bag.""

Solomon, "An inheritance gained hurriedly in the beginning will not be blessed in the end." (Proverbs 20:21)

Bequests that stifle a child's initiative, inhibit the development of God-given talents, rob them of self-confidence, burden them with the guilt of having too much, create a barrier to developing deep relationships, and propagate a false sense of security in their wealth. This is a curse to that child. Inherited wealth affects an ambitious overachiever differently than a spendthrift. Each individual's needs and unique circumstances must be carefully considered. One size does not fit all.

Solomon also said, "A good man leaves an inheritance for his children's children." (Proverbs13:22) This is absolutely true in terms of impeccable qualities of sterling character such as honesty, humility, contentment, love, joy, patience, kindness, goodness, faithfulness, gentleness, and self-control. "The greatest legacy one can pass on to children and grandchildren is not money or other material things accumulated in one's life but rather a legacy of character and faith." Billy Graham

It is also true with regard to "keep sakes," things with sentimental family value, as well as some things of monetary value. The Proverbs are true statements, but they are general statements. The beginning three or four chapters of Proverbs are about wisdom and how to get it. Parents are to impart wisdom to their children. One aspect of teaching wisdom has to do with the management of wealth and the value of diligence. Passing "valuables without values" can be detrimental to your heirs. Only you can determine the financial legacy that you will leave to your children, but it should be an appropriate amount, and it should be specific.

In addition, fair is not necessarily equal, and equal is not necessarily fair. In most situations parents are right to try to make equal bequests to their children, but where the facts and circumstances dictate a distribution of assets in a manner other than equal, parents should be courageous and make decisions that are right and reasonable.

Teach your children these eternal principles from Proverbs.

Proverbs 3

> [9]Honor the LORD with your wealth,
> with the first-fruits of all your crops;
> [10]then your barns will be filled to overflowing,
> and your vats will brim over with new wine.

Proverbs 6

> [10]A little sleep, a little slumber,
> a little folding of the hands to rest-
> [11]and poverty will come on you like a vagrant
> and scarcity like a beggar.

7 RECOMMENDATIONS

Transfer Wisdom Before Transferring Wealth

"A child is a person who is going to carry on what you started. A child is going to sit where you're sitting, and when you are gone, attend to those things which you think are important...He or she will assume control of your cities, states, and nations. Is going to move in and take over your churches, schools, universities, and corporations...The fate of humanity is in his or her hands. Teach them well!" – Abraham Lincoln

Lincoln exhorts us to teach our children well! Moses instructs us to impress God's commandments, his eternal principles, on our children when we sit at home, when we walk along the road, when we lie down, and when we rise up. Write them indelibly upon their minds! (Deuteronomy 6:4-9)

Leaving no money but passing values to heirs is acceptable. They likely will manage their lives very well. Leaving money and passing values to heirs is usually a positive situation. They just may change the world. Leaving money to heirs who have poorly developed values is asking for trouble.

If you want to know how they will treat an inheritance, then take a careful look at how they manage their money. Your heirs will manage your money the way they manage their money, not the way you manage your money.

We are all stewards of God's assets and we will each stand before the Lord and give an accounting of how we used the assets that he entrusted to us. Choose the next steward wisely and make sure that you and your spouse are in agreement on these important decisions.

Love Them Equally But Treat Them Uniquely

Parents should love their children equally and treat them uniquely. The differences in children – age, gender, temperament, physical and mental capability, demonstrated ability to handle money, spiritual commitment, spiritual maturity, economic status – must be considered. Entrusting God's resources to a slothful child, an ungodly child, a stingy child, or a spendthrift child is not wise. Obviously, such decisions are very hard and are fraught with great emotion. Treating our children differently just does not feel right, but, you are a steward and are accountable before God. He will expect you to make wise decisions.

Four Practices Designed to Inculcate Principles of Stewardship in Your Children

In the process of becoming a mature Christian we grow in our faith, in our knowledge of the Word, in our ability to communicate the good news, in our sincerity, and in our love for all mankind. To be complete in maturity, Paul declares that we must "also excel in this grace of giving." (2 Corinthians 8:7) Why is Christian giving integral to Christian maturity? Because the primary purpose of Christian giving is learning to put God first in every area of life.

There are three institutions that should be teaching and modeling Christian Stewardship – the church, Christian schools, and the family. It should be the purpose of each of these institutions to develop mature disciples of Christ with God's Word at the center. But, experience reveals that Christian schools are virtually silent on teaching stewardship, preachers avoid the topic, and most families are ill equipped to teach the subject, but there are exceptions. Most of those who practice generous giving have learned that way of life through the example of generous parents.

Giving, whether from our current income or from our estates, is a learned behavior. It comes from family values and it is not driven by capacity to give. Love for the Lord and doing good for others should be the primary motivating factors.

1. Model Stewardship Values. From birth, our natural tendency is to be self-centered. Typically, children are reluctant to share but quick to grasp their toys and say "mine." When a child grows up in a home where stewardship principles are taught and practiced, those early selfish tendencies are replaced with humility, kindness and generosity. Albert Schweitzer said, "There are three ways to teach a child. The first is by example, the second is by example, and the third is by example."

It comes back to lifestyle choices. Do we display a materialistic focus or a heart full of thanksgiving to God for blessing us so bountifully? Our house and our car – what do they say about whether our investment is in the heavenly kingdom or our earthly kingdom? Are we frugal and do we live within our means? Calvin Coolidge once said, "There is no dignity quite so impressive, and no independence quite so important, as living within your means." When we make stewardship decisions, we should include our children.

2. You Get Money from Working. We live in the age of the lottery, television game shows, and advertising that tells us that money comes easy and real life is found in the material things we own. Children must be taught that God worked, that Jesus worked and He expects his disciples to work hard, with all our heart, to go the second-mile, to provide for our family, and to give of our "first-fruits" to those in need.

3. Create a Lifestyle that Encourages Giving. Living within your means (not spending more than you earn) and promoting savings to give to God creates a lifestyle that is basic to a mature steward. An erroneous financial theory of our time is the notion that to make ends meet we need to make more money. But, an increase in earnings leads to an increase in our standard of living. That creates the vicious cycle that many Americans are on. There is nothing wrong with earning more money especially when our goal is to increase our standard of giving rather than our standard of living. The way to live within your means is to learn to live off less. This begins with giving and saving off the top of your income. One way to teach this principle to our children is to encourage them to deposit within a container the top 10% or more for making contributions to the Lord, and the next 10% or more in another container for savings, and to use wisely the balance.

4. Giving is a Habit. There is no better way and no better place to learn a good habit than by example in the home. Teaching children to save to give, to live as inexpensively as possible, and to include them in the family charitable giving decisions is a tremendous way to train mature stewards. A family meeting in which these things are discussed – work, income, expenses, making eternal investments, making temporal investments, seeking gift opportunities for advancing the cause of Christ, making decisions concerning gifts, and praying over each gift – is a moving experience and creates an indelible memory. Our children are watching and learning.

8 WHAT WILL YOU DO WITH YOUR ESTATE?

For Christians, being financially responsible begins with an examination of the Word of God and ends with obedience to the Word of God. "Keep this Book of the Law always on your lips; meditate on it day and night, so that you may be careful to do everything written in it. Then you will be prosperous and successful." (Joshua 1:8) Being financially responsible before the Lord is essential for Christians because Christians are stewards or managers of the assets entrusted to them by the heavenly Father. How money and possessions are handled lies at the very heart of the Christian life.

No one can tell you precisely what it means for you to be "rich toward God." Everyone's circumstances are unique. However, when contemplating your situation, it is wise to remember that scripture does not say to be rich toward your spouse or rich toward your children, but it does say to be rich toward God. How are we to be rich toward God?

1. By making generous gifts from your current income,

expecting nothing in return, to those in need, to the church, and to organizations that advance the Lord's work in this world,

2.By executing an estate plan through which you commit generous bequests to the church and to organizations that advance the Lord's kingdom by supporting local and foreign missions, children's homes, inner city ministries, disaster relief, faith-based counseling, Christian education, or any other good work that brings honor and glory to Christ Jesus and his church,

3.By refusing to place your hope, your trust in riches but in the one who richly provides all of our needs through the riches of his glory,

4.By looking at the assets entrusted to you through the lens of eternity.

What are you giving to Jesus through your estate to show your love for Him? Scripture teaches clearly that we are to love Jesus more than family. We teach our children to love Jesus, and we declare to our children that we love Jesus. Is it consistent to declare that we love Jesus and then to exclude Jesus from our estate plan?

What did God do when he wanted to show his love for you? Did he lean over the parapets of heaven and say for the whole world to hear, "I want you to know that I love you down there. I really do love you!" And then,